Series Editor Nigel Trevena

Published by
ATLANTIC TRANSPORT PUBLISHERS
Waterside House   Falmouth Road
Penryn   Cornwall   TR10 8BE   England

Volume Four

The LNER Pacifics

by P. N. TOWNEND

Designed by Nigel Trevena
Printed by Century Litho, Penryn, Cornwall

© P. N. Townend and accredited photographers

No part of this publication may be reproduced in any form or by any means without the prior written permission of the publishers

ISBN 0 906899 14 1   First published 1985
                     Reprinted 1988

Acknowledgements

For every hundred good black and white photographs of the LNER Pacifics there are, in my experience, perhaps two or three in colour: a reminder that railway colour photography only became established in the late 1950s when colour film of serviceable speed became available. Even then, only a small minority of photographers experimented with the new medium.

This has meant that the compilation of a colour book on *any* British steam locomotive is fraught with difficulties. The fact that we have overcome most of these in this book — with coverage of all the classes of LNER Pacific, a good spread of individual variations and a tantalising glimpse of *real* LNER liveries — is due entirely to the generous contributions of all the photographers whose names are recorded in these pages. My sincere thanks to them all, particularly to Dick Riley and Peter Hughes who provided so much fine material, and to the ever enthusiastic Ron White at Colour-Rail.

One or two studies have been included more for their historical significance than their technical excellence and, because of their contractual obligations, all photographs credited to Colour-Rail have been reproduced from duplicate, rather than original, transparencies.

It has been a pleasure and privilege to work with Peter Townend. Peter's knowledge of the LNER Pacifics is unrivalled and his detailed and absorbing captions lift this volume of *The Colour of Steam* far above the level of the ordinary picture book. My thanks to Peter, and I trust the book stirs a few memories of the days when *real* locomotives worked in Britain.

Nigel Trevena Series Editor

FRONT COVER: A3 No.60039 *Sandwich* at Kings Cross Top Shed after receiving the German type smoke deflectors in 1961. The double chimney had been fitted in 1959 at a cost of £153: this very minor expenditure at a general overhaul then costing over £5,000 put the A3s back onto any of the fastest workings on the East Coast main line. Return workings to Newcastle and back in a little over 12 hours, in place of diesels not available, became commonplace. Such long workings with little time for shed work had not been attempted before the diesels came along and resulted in some high mileages over short periods, enabling the changeover to diesel traction to proceed without difficulty. *Photo: P. N. Townend*

BACK COVER: A4 No.60031 *Golden Plover* waiting to leave Glasgow Queen Street station with the up 'Queen of Scots' Pullman on 13th May 1961. The train was banked out to Cowlairs by North British 0-6-2T No.69163 in accordance with normal practice. *Golden Plover* was a regularly manned Haymarket engine for nearly 25 years before being transferred to St Rollox depot in 1962 where it spent its last three years working the Glasgow to Aberdeen expresses.

Note the porthole visible at the back of the tender providing the only light inside the corridor tender, which was generally full of fire irons. *Golden Plover* ran with a middle cylinder reduced in diameter to 17" 1947-59. Six liners were made but only five were used in an attempt to equalise the work done in the three cylinders and counteract any overtravel due to the use of the conjugated valve gear. No tests were made to measure the work done in the middle cylinder of an A4 either before or after fitting but an A1 class engine was indicated and although fitted with independent valve gear the middle cylinder was found to have a considerable disparity in work done between the front and back strokes. This was found to be due to the expansion of the frames which would not occur on the A4 where the cylinders were in line. In the end the conjugated Gresley valve gear gave no trouble in service but the inside eccentric fitted to the later Pacifics did occasionally fail on the road resulting in the engine having to be removed from its train.
Photo: M. Mensing

TITLE PAGE: In Scotland, the A4s had their swansong when at the request of the General Manager, James Ness, the remaining engines were used from 1962 to 1966 for operating the sharply timed three hour expresses between Glasgow and Aberdeen over the former Caledonian main line. It was a canny move as the A4s had the edge over the heavy diesel electric locos available and could improve on the sectional timings. No.60004 *William Whitelaw* is seen here taking water at Perth station whilst working the 17.30 Glasgow to Aberdeen express in July 1963. The name of the Chairman of the LNER had been upgraded from the first of the NBL built A1s to an A4 in 1941.
Photo: Hughes Junction

LEFT: A1 No.60123 *H.A. Ivatt* on the up 'Yorkshire Pullman' at Gamston in May 1961.
Photo: Hughes Junction

ABOVE: Close up on *Flying Scotsman*.
Photo: H.G. Forsythe

Introduction

It was my good fortune to live as a boy before the war in Doncaster where the giants of the LNER could be seen every day in excellent form and every train was worked by steam. The achievements of the LNER Pacifics were headline news in the national as well as local newspapers, very often accompanied by a half page photograph of the train concerned or some new locomotive from Doncaster Works. Much of the population of the town turned out to man every vantage point and see the 'Silver Jubilee' sweep through the station at nearly 70 mph with a long blast on the chime whistle of *Silver Link* on the inaugural run heading north. The Pacifics all carried names and what an inspired collection they were with cities, racehorses and birds strong on the wing. Somehow, the later policy to introduce names of directors did not seem to fit an engine at the head of a 16 coach train the same as *Peregrine* or *Royal Lancer*.

1939 brought an abrupt end to an epoch and things were never to be quite the same again. The local Garter Blue A4s were carefully stored inside the shed at Doncaster to await better times, but it was soon necessary to put them back to work. The Pacifics and V2s proved the value of Gresley's big engine policy and could be seen daily at the head of trains over 20 coaches in length, without assistance. After the war, in a period of drabness, the LNER quickly restored the Pacifics to their former colours of blue and green, but there was little opportunity to display their pre-war running potential on the rundown railway which remained. Strange looking Pacifics appeared but eventually these different ideas were tidied up into the most powerful and reliable A1 and A2 classes, of which the five A1s with roller bearings to all the axles must surely represent the culmination of the art of designing the LNER Pacifics at Doncaster.

Alas, the unbelievable happened and within a short period the LNER Pacifics had all been withdrawn, many not half way through their normal lifespan. But not quite all went to the scrapheap: a very small select few can still be seen at work, not on their home ground but nevertheless providing the sights, sounds and smell that small boys and many much older enjoyed on every mainline train that once passed by on the LNER.

I am indeed grateful to those photographers who changed their film and cameras to use colour, persevering with the difficulties in order to record the scene and therefore make this book possible. My particular thanks are due to Nigel Trevena who tracked down the colour transparencies which in turn have brought back memories of some of the finest locomotives to run in this country.

P. N. Townend

THE LNER PACIFICS
Express Passenger Locomotives
Wheel 4-6-2   Cylinders 3

Class	Designer	Year Intro	Weight Loco	Weight Non-corridor tender	Pressure lb sq in	Cylinder	Driving Wheel	Tractive Effort lbs	Total Engines	Withdrawn
A3	Gresley	1927	96t 5c	57t 18c	220	19" x 26"	6'8"	32,909	78	12.59 – 1.66
A4	Gresley	1935	102t 19c	60t 7c	250	18½" x 26"	6'8"	35,455	35	12.62 – 9.66
A2/2	Thompson	1943	101t 10c	60t 7c	225	20" x 26"	6'2"	40,318	6	11.59 – 7.61
A2/1	Thompson	1944	98t 0c	52t 0c or 60t 7c	225	19" x 26"	6'2"	36,387	4	8.60 – 2.61
A2/3	Thompson	1946	101t 10c	60t 7c	250	19" x 26"	6'2"	40,430	15	11.62 – 6.65
A1/1	Thompson	1945	101t 10c	57t 18c	250	19" x 26"	6'8"	37,397	1	11.62
A2	Peppercorn	1947	101t 0c	60t 7c	250	19" x 26"	6'2"	40,430	15	11.62 – 12.66
A1	Peppercorn	1948	104t 2c	60t 7c	250	19" x 26"	6'8"	37,397	49	10.62 – 6.66

Roller bearing engines slightly heavier

LEFT: A4 No.60025 *Falcon* on an up car carrier near Dukeries Junction in July 1962. *Photo: Hughes Junction*

Twilight of the LNER

Sir Hugo resplendent in LNER apple green livery again after almost five years in wartime black. This Newcastle A3 was waiting to leave Grantham and was the first of the Pacifics to be restored to the pre-war standard green. Only two engines received this with their original numbers and No.2582 was altered to 83 two months later in October 1946.
Photo: C. C. B. Herbert, via R. C. Riley

A3

A3 livery variations

LEFT: A3 class No.60084 *Trigo* at Newcastle station on 20th August 1948. This engine had been painted three months earlier in an experimental blue/purple colour with cream and red lining out, quite a different blue to that adopted in May 1949 as the BR standard livery. *Trigo* was always a North Eastern area locomotive and was painted in five different colours in just over 5½ years, changing from wartime black to LNER green in 1947, to blue/purple in 1948, to BR standard blue in 1949 and to BR standard green in 1952. *Photo: H. N. James/ Colour-Rail*

RIGHT: The incorrectly named A3 class No.60065 *Knight of Thistle* at Haymarket depot late in 1949. A 'the' was missing after new plates were cast in 1932. The engine was photographed shortly after receiving the BR standard blue livery with black and white lining and the early 'hungry lion' BR crest. The blue was standard on the A3s from May 1949 to August 1951, a colour in my view not worn comfortably. This locomotive still retains right hand drive, note the vacuum exhaust pipe along the side of the boiler. It was not converted to left hand drive until December 1952 when the engine was also changed to BR green livery. *Photo: J. Robertson/Colour-Rail*

LEFT: A3 class No.60060 *The Tetrarch* at Kings Cross Top Shed in September 1961. Note the higher sides of the new type non-corridor tender fitted to this engine and the orange and black lining out with Brunswick green livery used from 1951. Although fitted with a Kylchap double chimney in March 1959 and not withdrawn until September 1963 this locomotive never received the smoke deflectors authorised in March 1961. *The Tetrarch* was, however, fitted with an A4 boiler, but working at 220lbs sq inch, one of the 36 to do so from 1954. This can be recognised by the longer combustion chamber apparent in this photograph. The change was not specially advised to depots with the result that, on the first occasion new superheater elements were required, the longer A3 pattern were ordered. *Photo: R. C. Riley*

BELOW: One of the pleasures arising from the preservation of steam locomotives is to see engines at work in the full glory of their former liveries, often far away from their normal line of route covered when in everyday use. *Flying Scotsman* shows the detail of its LNER standard green with black, white and red lining out here on the Torbay Steam Railway at Kingswear. *Photo: P. N. Townend*

A3s in traffic

A busy Kings Cross station scene photographed in June 1959, with A3 No.60067 *Ladas* in the station loco depot and an A1 leaving on a down express. It was the practice to use the station loco plant to ensure the quality of coal, and that it was properly broken up, for engines working the 'Elizabethan'. Other locomotives, such as visitors working with their crews back to their home sheds, were also coaled there to save time, in preference to calling at Top Shed. Practically everything in the view except the station has gone forever, including the Baby Deltic diesel locomotive making its contribution to the smoke. The station and the track layout have also been considerably altered. *Photo: T. B. Owen/ Colour-Rail*

LEFT: A3 class No.60048 *Doncaster* near Brookmans Park on an up express from Newcastle in February 1959. The stock is painted in the so called 'blood and custard' colours of the early 1950s. The locomotive retains the Great Northern type eight wheeled tender which is displaying the later BR crest. The 'banjo', or more correctly the perforated steam collecting dome, was fitted to most of the A3s by then, as only a small batch of nine boilers made under the jurisdiction of E. Thompson in 1944 with round domes were still available. The first two 180lbs boilers steamed over a million miles each, albeit with new fireboxes and wrapper plates during this period, but the higher pressure A3 boilers did not achieve such mileages. Although appropriate for a Doncaster built engine to carry that name, the name in fact commemorates the racehorse which won the 1873 Derby. The locomotive was allocated to Doncaster for many years, but in February 1959 it was working from Grantham. *Photo: T. B. Owen/Colour-Rail*

BELOW: A3 No.60082 *Neil Gow* is making hard work of starting the up 'Thames Clyde Express' out of Glasgow St Enoch's station in April 1961. It is slipping badly and with many joints blowing it would not appear to be maintained in very good order. *Photo: G. T. Robinson/GTR Slides*

ABOVE: The down 'Thames Clyde Express' passing Shipley curve in May 1961 again worked by No.60082 *Neil Gow*. Although the A3s had been successfully tried over the former Midland Railway Ais Gill route in 1954, it was not until 1960 that regular workings commenced with 8 of these engines being allocated to Holbeck depot, Leeds. After the crews had got used to handling LNER Pacifics there is no doubt the fireman had an easier time. The fitting of the double Kylchap blastpipe to the A3 had saved about 6lbs of coal per mile as well as producing a freer steaming engine. A wide firebox could also be well filled in the back corners before leaving the shed but there was a knack in getting coal through the LNER half trap firehole door when the engine was working without burning your hands.
Photo: Gavin Morrison

LEFT: *Sir Frederick Banbury*, then the oldest surviving LNER Pacific, entering Kings Cross station in 1961, appropriately with some Gresley stock behind the tender. After No.4470 *Great Northern* had been rebuilt in 1945 this Pacific, named after the last chairman of the GNR, was the only Great Northern built survivor. It was withdrawn that November, only 2½ years after receiving a double chimney. It must be

pointed out, however, particularly in the case of these early Pacifics, that practically everything had been renewed as necessary and sometimes several times in a life of nearly 40 years. This was not so with the later Pacifics which retained their original frames.
Photo: Colour/Rail

No.60064 *Tagalie* leaving Grantham on a Kings Cross to Leeds express in May 1960. It was fitted with a double chimney in 1959 but it was withdrawn in 1961 before receiving smoke deflectors. This engine was named *William Whitelaw* until 1941 and was a rarity south of the border until transferred to Doncaster in 1950 and in 1959 to Grantham. The transfer from Scotland was made due to complaints from the drivers' representatives as the locomotive had retained right hand drive. It was altered to left hand, which was the standard side for signals, in 1953.
Photo: Hughes Junction

Smoke deflector A3s

TOP: The up 'Talisman' leaving Newcastle at King Edward Bridge Junction in June 1960 with Gateshead depot in the distance. The A3 locomotive No.60055 *Woolwinder* was the first to be changed to a Kylchap double blastpipe after the war and the small wing-type smoke deflectors fitted to the top of the smokebox were added the following year in 1959. It was the first of four to be fitted experimentally.

After fitting the double blastpipes to all the A3s between 1958 and 1960 it became necessary to fit smoke deflectors due to the very low pressure of the exhaust steam drifting down along the boiler and obliterating the driver's view of signals. It was therefore necessary to do something about it quickly and Doncaster was asked to fit smoke deflectors. Much testing of various forms of smokebox shapes and deflectors had been tried by Doncaster for some years before the war and these tests had culminated in the streamlined front of the A4 and none of the small deflectors tried had been satisfactory.

Woolwinder and *Pretty Polly* were two engines fitted in 1959 with these small deflectors and as they were allocated to Kings Cross I was asked to report upon their effectiveness at regular intervals. In view of the limited life of the locomotives it was necessary to conclude the experiment quickly and the authorities were therefore reminded of the pre-war tests which had been fully reported to the Institution of Locomotive Engineers by the Chief Draughtsman at Doncaster, E. Windle. These tests had concluded that the only satisfactory solution found was the streamlined front adopted on the A4. The P2 class was changed to this shape for that reason and the new A1 class ordered by the LNER before nationalisation were also intended to be similarly streamlined. There was no likelihood of the A3s being streamlined at this stage and it was suggested that as the German railways were changing their previous design of full size deflectors on hundreds of engines to a new type attached only to the smokebox that it might be worthwhile trying this pattern instead. A side view photograph of a German 01 class Pacific I had taken in Cologne station was submitted with the offer that I would try them if a set could be supplied. Within a few weeks a drawing was sent for checking and the fitting of four locomotives at Doncaster authorised. *Galtee More* of Grantham was the first fitted, in October 1960, and it was loaned to Kings Cross for a week and tested on the 10.00 am 'Flying Scotsman', a diesel diagram through to Newcastle and back with the 17.05 due into Kings Cross at 22.10, a round working of 536 miles in a little over 12 hours. A different inspector was used on each day and in over 3,000 miles running the total time the driver's vision was obscured was 25 seconds.
Photo: J. P. Mullet/Colour Rail

LEFT, BOTTOM: No.60042 *Singapore* is seen descending Dunblane bank with the up 'Grampian' in May 1964, two months before withdrawal. It was built as an A3 in 1934, one of the last batch which were built new with steam collector 'banjo' domes. This engine spent all its life allocated to the North Eastern section until being sent to Scotland in 1963. The plate fitted behind the screw coupling from 1953 was to prevent the coupling swinging and damaging the Automatic Warning System receiver below.
Photo: A. E. R. Cope/Colour-Rail

A3 No.60107 *Royal Lancer* is leaving Markham tunnel on a Leeds to Kings Cross express. The smoke deflectors can be seen to be working effectively. This engine survived until 1963 having completed 40 years service and just over 2¼ million miles. That was a sad year for the Gresley A3s as 33 were withdrawn and Top Shed closed. An April 1962 picture.
Photo: Hughes Junction

A3s on shed; at works

A3 class No.60067 *Ladas* at Top Shed, Kings Cross, shortly after being fitted at the depot with German type smoke deflectors in 1961. Although the A3s were now in splendid form, this engine was scrapped at the end of 1962 when due for repair. The policy of updating at a minimum cost the oldest locomotives did however enable the Line Manager to continue to improve the East Coast main line services throughout the protracted changeover to diesel traction and the Pacifics then had perhaps their finest hour.
Photo: P. N. Townend

TOP: A3 No.60044 *Melton* and A1 No.60128 *Bongrace* are standing outside the weighhouse at Doncaster Works in September 1962. 'The Plant' at Doncaster built many of the Pacifics and maintained the whole fleet from 1930 until November 1963 except for the handful of Raven engines. From the late 1950s the Kings Cross A3 and A4 locomotives were also given valves and pistons examinations in Doncaster Works in order to ease the work load at the depot where recruitment of skilled staff was very difficult and working conditions primitive to say the least. At this examination, carried out at 36,000 mile intervals, the driving pair of axleboxes were also renewed whilst all the rods were down: a local arrangement in order to avoid the right driving axlebox running hot due to excessive crown wear towards one side. It had been found that this side axlebox was at risk at mileages higher than this. The axleboxes had also become non-standard once the Swindon practice of optically aligning the cylinders to the frames had been adopted at Doncaster: this resulted in delays in obtaining new axleboxes which had to be machined to the last optical alignment measurements. This problem only occurred on Gresley locomotives where the three cylinders drove onto the same axle and hot driving axleboxes were virtually unknown on the later A1 and A2 varieties, with the exception of 5 A1 class fitted with a non-standard divided axlebox. The arrangement with the works operated very well indeed enabling high mileages to be run between general repairs and improving the maintenance of the Pacifics at a critical time. The building behind the tender of No.60044 is where the locomotive was weighed after work's attention and the weight on each spring individually adjusted. No.60044 was a Kings Cross engine and probably in works for valves and pistons examination. *Photo: Gavin Morrison*

BOTTOM: No.60045 *Lemberg* at Darlington in May 1964 where the engine spent its last months, until withdrawal that November, as main line pilot, being used when required to replace any failed traction unit. *Lemberg* was converted to class A3 in 1927 by replacing the original 180lbs boiler with one at 220lbs pressure. This increased the weight of the locomotive but by then a 22 ton axle load was permitted. The additional tractive effort was required for working over the gradients of the Edinburgh to Carlisle line but Gresley was concerned about the increased cost of maintaining higher pressure boilers. At the same time, longer travel valves were fitted and *Lemberg* alone had the cylinders lined up to 18¼" in order to equate the tractive effort of the lower pressure engines for trial purposes. A Doncaster engine until 1937, its regular driver considered it the fastest thing on wheels. *Photo: J. Richardson*

Early A4 liveries

BELOW: A very important photograph of the first A4, No.2509 *Silver Link*, on the up 'Flying Scotsman' in Grantham station in June 1937. The locomotive is painted in silver grey, battleship grey and dark charcoal, unlined, with the name painted on the boiler side. When first painted the silver grey came to a point at the front but this was changed before entering service to the more effective parabolic curve. Nameplates were also initially fitted but quickly removed. The handrail over the firebox was originally straight but the last pillar was later dropped. On *Silver Link* the curve did not match the footplating as it did on the later builds.

No new locomotive started work so spectacularly as did *Silver Link*. Within a few days of completion in 1935 the engine had pushed the world record to 112½ mph and covered 43 miles at an average of 100 mph. Although the record high speeds, achieved with the help of gravity, caught the public's attention such speeds were not necessary in the everyday operation of the streamlined trains. The real achievement of the A4 class was in their uphill running at speeds approaching and later exceeding 70 mph on the long 1 in 200 gradients of the East Coast main line.

The success, reliability and economy of the A4s which made the operation of the high speed trains possible was due to the painstaking attention of Gresley and his technical staff at Doncaster to the design details of the original A1 Pacific from 1922. The A4's shape was derived from the horizontal wedge of the French Bugatti railcars and all the stipulations of the running department for safety and access were successfully embodied.
Photo: J. A. Whaley/Colour-Rail

ABOVE, LEFT: No.4498 *Sir Nigel Gresley* is waiting to leave Darlington station with an up express in August 1938. This was the 100th Pacific to be constructed when completed in November 1937 and appropriately named after its designer, then held in very high esteem by the LNER and the public. It was painted in the Garter Blue livery of the four Coronation locomotives which had by then been adopted for the whole class. The bright metal numbers and letters were only applied to selected locomotives and transfers were used on *Sir Nigel Gresley*. Although the A4 class was designed for working the streamlined trains, many of the class were actually built for working the heavy East Coast expresses and No.4498 was the last of an order built with Government financial aid to reduce the number of unemployed. Happily, this locomotive is one of six A4s preserved and can still be seen regularly working special trains on BR. *Photo: Colour-Rail*

ABOVE, RIGHT: *Dwight D. Eisenhower*, by now No.8, leaving the loop at Sandy on an up parcels train on 26th August 1948. This engine was the first to be restored to Garter Blue in September 1945 but it was not renumbered 8 until November 1946. Although it was some months before the remainder of the A4s commenced receiving the blue livery with Coronation red wheels and red and white lining applied to the smokebox curve, the restoration to pre-war splendour was carried out quickly in the rather austere period after the war. When I was Shedmaster at Kings Cross from 1956 the A4s were still always affectionately called by drivers 'blue uns' despite having been painted green for many years. The valancing below the footplating was removed during the war in order to ease inspection and maintenance accessibility but was not replaced (except on *Mallard* when preserved).
Photo: H. N. James/Colour-Rail

BELOW: *Mallard*, now numbered E22, is waiting to leave Waterloo for Exeter in June 1948, during the comprehensive Locomotive Exchanges organised by BR. The Kylchap A4s used throughout the Interchange Trials produced the lowest coal and water consumption figures of the tests, although not nominally the most powerful of the passenger engines tested, an A4 produced the highest drawbar pull at speed when accelerating a 350 ton train up Hemerdon bank to 24 mph. The trials also highlighted some problems with the middle big end bearing and *Mallard* had to be replaced when this overheated whilst working on the Southern Region. After adding a strengthening rib to the strap, alterations to the lubrication and a change to a thin white metal bearing surface accurately machined, the middle big end ceased to be a problem in later years.
Photo: C. C. B. Herbert via R. C. Riley

RIGHT: *Mallard* on exhibition at Noel Park on 13th September 1958. The display was arranged to celebrate the 750th anniversary of the granting of a charter to the Borough of Wood Green. The locomotives were prepared by the two Top Shed chargehand cleaners Dick Ball and Harry Frost with much help from the paint brush of Frank Rayner who served his time at Melton Constable. Although several new diesel locomotives were on view, it was *Mallard* which had a long queue to pass through the cab, with one question everyone required answering — what train was it next working out of Kings Cross?

BELOW: Numbered 4468, *Mallard* at Nine Elms depot in February 1964 en route from Doncaster to Clapham Museum of British Transport with the crossheads disconnected. The locomotive had been withdrawn in April 1963 and with only very minor exceptions was restored to its original appearance, complete with valancing. She was the first of four A4s to be constructed with double Kylchap blastpipes in March 1938 which enabled the world speed record to be raised to 125 mph. The plaque commemorating this fact was not placed on the sides of the engine until 1948, just after nationalisation, after some correspondance from enthusiasts as to why the locomotive did not display anything to commemorate the event. The speed on the plaque is 126 mph which Gresley himself did not claim and this peak could only have been attained over a few yards.
Photos: R. C. Riley

LEFT: The LNER Pacifics were used for working many important trains during their lifetime but the last great Royal occasion was in June 1961 when three A4s were turned out by Kings Cross for the special trains to York and back from Malton on the occasion of the wedding of the Duke of Kent. The Queen and the Royal Family travelled on their own in the Royal Train; two other trains carried the Prime Minister and other important State representatives and guests. No.60003 *Andrew K. McCosh* was used on one of these and all the locomotives had the visible metalwork shining with white cab roofs. Although diesels were available, the decision was taken at the highest level to use steam. All the locomotives used completed the workings without any difficulties, regaining late starts on the return journey to arrive at Kings Cross before time. Next day the Line Manager invited all those who had participated, from the crews to the Shedmaster, to his office to sample a firkin of beer which he had placed on his desk. *Andrew K. McCosh* is seen here being prepared at Top Shed on 17th June 1961.
Photo: R. C. Riley

A4s in traffic

RIGHT: A4 No.60030 *Golden Fleece* entering Kings Cross at Belle Isle on 18th March 1961. The North London line still crosses the Great Northern at this point but the throat has now been rationalised and the signalboxes and the two nearside tracks have disappeared. *Golden Fleece*, originally used on the streamlined 'West Riding Limited' before the war, has polished buffers which were fitted and kept bright on many A4s allocated to Kings Cross. An electric warning flash is conspicuous on the side of the smokebox and the leading vehicle of the train is one of the LNER steel sided Newton coaches with elliptically shaped toilet windows. The doors of the coach are away from the ends to help overcome the considerable congestion experienced in wartime with end doors.
Photo: R. C. Riley

An A4 in close-up: No.60008 at Top Shed

TOP: No.60008 is backing down for coal before leaving the shed at Kings Cross in October 1961. The coal hopper held 500 tons of coal and was filled once a day with wagons hauled up the side and turned over at the top into either of two bunkers. One man could fill the bunkers on a day turn whereas 12 to 18 men would be required to work around the clock previously. The practice of going back for coal was discouraged as the movement clashed with other engines arriving on the depot and caused late departures. The crew would make the fire up on the front of the shed and the engine drop down towards the outlet signal. If the Running Foreman was not looking, the locomotive would be back under the coaling plant to fill the front of the tender: the coal on the back rarely got used! The red background to the nameplate was a local arrangement at Top Shed, which resulted in official disapproval as someone complained to the CME that the colour did not contrast well on the panchromatic film of the day making the name difficult to read on a photograph! *Photo: J. P. Mullett/Colour-Rail*

BOTTOM: *Dwight D. Eisenhower* with *Dominion of New Zealand* alongside on the back pits at Kings Cross depot in June 1962. Both have their cod's mouth open. It was one of the design stipulations that any doors which opened must not be beyond the gauge line of the footplate and another stated that if any casing was put round the front of the smokebox it should be possible to open it from the ground level. The bottom section let down and was held by chains but the top part was operated by a key inserted below the footplating at the front and wound up or down. The inspiration for this feature came to the draughtsman concerned as he went home to lunch passing the Doncaster Corporation refuse cart on the way, which included the mechanism required. No front footsteps were ever provided on the A4 class. The streamlined shape only became effective for clearing the exhaust when the depression behind the chimney was made on a wind tunnel model *by mistake*. The previous straight line from the chimney to the boiler top of the P2, which was being used, did not clear the exhaust from the driver's vision.
Photo: J. P. Mullett/Colour-Rail

ABOVE: At Top Shed shortly after receiving the Kylchap double blastpipe in 1958. The engine is in back gear. Note the neat arrangement of the front and back valve crosshead guides, also the three slidebar arrangement used by Gresley for the crosshead. The photograph was arranged for an American enthusiast Thomas T. Taber and a print duly sent to the President.

The fitting of the Kylchap double blastpipes in 1957-1958 to all the single chimney A4s was achieved after many years of juggling the dimensions inside the smokebox, none of which could equate or provide the efficiency of the Kylchap arrangement. It had been known from the tests at Vitry commissioned by the LNER that an increase in the blastpipe orificial area reduced the back pressure from the cylinders and enhanced the power available at the drawbar. The cross-sectional area of the blastpipes had been compared in a table for all the express locomotives in the Interchange Trial Report of 1948 and the double chimney A4 had by far the greatest area of any of the locomotives tested. The arrangement of the Kylchap cowls inside the smokebox also increased the steaming capacity of the engine by spreading the draught more evenly across the tubeplate and increasing the smokebox vacuum which helped to overcome any minor deficiencies in maintenance. Gresley had decreed after the success of *Mallard* that all new Pacifics should be fitted but took no retrospective action, no doubt due to the high costs involved whilst still covered by the patent rights. E. Thompson fitted the arrangement to all the Pacifics built or rebuilt but in the 1950s there was considerable resistance to fitting any more. In a determined effort to have the benefits on *all* the Pacifics allocated to Kings Cross, including 16 A4s not fitted, comparative coal consumption trials were carried out locally with single and double chimney locomotives from Kings Cross to Doncaster and back, carefully weighing the coal used. A saving of about 6 to 7 lbs of coal per mile was sufficient to persuade the General Manager to ask Doncaster to fit all the A4s quickly, which were then followed by the A3s, giving the East Coast route one of the largest fleets of Kylchap fitted express passenger engines in Europe, and at a minimum cost.
Photo: P. N. Townend

A4s in action

No.60013 *Dominion of New Zealand* working a Leeds to Kings Cross express very easily on Gamston bank in August 1961. It was fitted with a double chimney in July 1958, which considerably enhanced its steaming capacity and improved its reliability over the last five years before withdrawal. The whistle fitted was from the New Zealand Government Railways and had the deepest note and least attractive sound of any of the A4 whistles.

Dominion of New Zealand was one of four A4s selected and appropriately named for working the Coronation streamlined train between Edinburgh and Kings Cross, on a six hour timing including stops, in July 1937. The schedule from Kings Cross to York initially demanded an average speed of 71·9 mph, the highest speed required in any timetable in this country up to that time. *Photo: Hughes Junction*

RIGHT: In 1928, the LNER gained much prestige and publicity by running the 10.00 am 'Flying Scotsman' non-stop between London and Edinburgh in both directions from May to September. Although initially the locomotive work was not demanding due to not reducing the timings in force, it was an endurance feat for the locomotive to travel 393 miles without an opportunity to check that everything was in order. The train ran every year until the war with reduced timings and from 1937 the A4s took over the workings. The period of operation was however shorter than in 1928.

In 1948 the non-stop was put back into service and ran every year during the height of the summer until 1961, worked solely by A4s which were the only engines fitted with corridor tenders. From the Coronation year of 1953 the train became 'The Elizabethan' and the timings had been reduced to 6½ hours by 1961. The engines were turned out daily in pristine condition by Haymarket and Kings Cross and it was rare indeed for any time to be booked to loco or any substitution be made en route. Perhaps the Gresley Pacifics should be best remembered for working the world's longest non-stop run so well over

the years. This September 1960 photograph shows No.60032 *Gannet* at Nene Bridge, Peterborough, on the up 'Elizabethan'. *Photo: J. P. Mullet/Colour Rail*

BELOW: No.60009 *Union of South Africa* working an Edinburgh to Aberdeen express near Carmont in July 1964. This was always a Scottish based locomotive and appropriately has been preserved in Scotland by Mr John Cameron. The plate fitted to the left hand boiler side depicts a springbok and was donated by a South African newspaper proprietor. *Photo: M. Mensing*

A2/1

RIGHT: No.60508 *Duke of Rothesay* on a down express at Markham summit in May 1960. It was withdrawn early the following year. The larger smoke deflectors improve the engine's appearance. This was one of the last four of an order for V2 class locomotives constructed by Thompson as Pacifics in 1944 to 1945 and eventually classified as A2/1. The rear part of the engine and the boiler were identical to the V2 but the front end was similar in layout to the P2 rebuilds. The main frames were, however, in one piece but also had to be strengthened eventually. The smaller V2 tenders originally fitted were replaced with eight wheel tenders, as seen here.
Photo: P. J. Hughes/Colour-Rail

A2/2

LEFT: No.60506 *Wolf of Badenoch* working an up express at Eaton Wood in August 1959. This engine was the only A2/2 not to receive a rimmed chimney but it had been fitted with a half round beading to the top edge. The P2s were rebuilt to Pacifics in wartime by the simple expedient of cutting off the front part of the 2-8-2 including the boiler and splicing on a new section of frames with new cylinders. The old front end of the first rebuilds were left on the Crimpsall bank for up to 17 months, after which the nameplates were retrieved and replaced on the rebuilds. These engines were altered by Thompson to gain experience of his ideas with a divided drive 3 cylinder locomotive, at a time when the availability of the P2s was poor and materials for new passenger locomotives hard to obtain. Oddly, the rebuild was designed round the rather short outside connecting rod which resulted in the somewhat unhappy looking appearance. Not only did it look wrong, but the front end arrangement gave rise to additional maintenance resulting in further strengthening of the frames between the outside and inside cylinders. There was,

however, no question of the locomotives not being able to do the work required of them, although on this cold morning a cloud of steam is leaking from the exhaust joints. *Photo: P. J. Hughes/Colour-Rail*

ABOVE: No.60501 *Cock o' the North* adjacent to the old coaling plant at Doncaster depot, 20th April 1958. It is now a Pacific class A2/2 after being rebuilt from a 2-8-2 class P2 in 1944 by Mr Edward Thompson. It was withdrawn in 1960 and the whole class had gone by the following year. The burnt patch on the smokebox door is the result of drawing air due to the door not fitting properly to the asbestos joint ring. The small smoke deflectors were of limited value and their purpose would be largely defeated by fitting the rimmed chimney. This type of chimney was fitted in place of the plain variety used by Thompson due to the BRB designers ribbing Doncaster that they could not design a decent chimney, ignoring the fact that the plain type was better for clearing smoke. *Photo: W. Potter*

A2/3

ABOVE: No.60523 *Sun Castle* passing Holloway on a parly to Peterborough in June 1963, the month it was withdrawn. Although New England depot to which this engine was allocated did not have much express work, their collection of the Thompson varieties were called upon at times to assist Kings Cross, particularly at weekends and holiday peaks. I remember one occasion when the Pacifics at Top Shed — all Gresley types at the time — were suffering from maintenance problems resulting in poor availability. I telephoned the Shedmaster at New England to borrow an engine for the 'Yorkshire Pullman', a Leeds lodge turn. *Owen Tudor* arrived, but did not suit the driver at all. I asked him to at least try the engine for me. On arrival back the next day the driver, rather pleased with himself, rang me from the station and asked if he could have it all the week as it was a 'good un'! Although the lovely signal gantry seen here has now gone the flyover is still used not just for access to the goods yard but by the electric multiple units entering Kings Cross suburban platforms.
Photo: D. M. C. Hepburne-Scott/Colour-Rail

RIGHT: No.60514 *Chamossaire* is taking coal at Kings Cross depot before returning to Peterborough where it spent most of its working life allocated to New England depot. It was photographed in June 1962 and withdrawn at the end of that year. The 15 class A2/3s were built new 1946-1947 and were more powerful than the V2 against which they were tested, to the extent of about 20%. These locomotives had therefore considerable potential with a dimensionally much improved front end design, but as trains became lighter the opportunity to display their power was rarely provided. An example did arise, however, late in their life when a very heavy block cement train diagrammed for a class 9F had difficulty in maintaining the sharp timing to Stoke summit. An A2/3 was sent out instead, with Peterborough Inspector Bill Buxton who reported back that it was the only locomotive to master the job.
Photo: J. P. Mullett/Colour-Rail

A2/3s in traffic

LEFT: The up 'Postal' is seen here near Carmont in September 1963 hauled by class A2/3 No.60524 *Herringbone*. The horse was a St Leger winner but to the casual traveller it must have appeared to be an odd name for a locomotive — unless he was a betting man! This engine was allocated to Polmadie depot for a year or so until withdrawal in 1965. The class lasted longer than many of the later built Pacifics and did not require as much attention in works as the earlier Thompson rebuilds.
Photo: D. M. C. Hepburne-Scott/Colour-Rail

A2/3 at Top Shed

No.60500 *Edward Thompson*, the 2,000th locomotive built at Doncaster Works, at Top Shed, 16th September 1961. It had been turned at the station depot as the shed turntable was being renewed. The turntables at both the station and the depot were replaced a few years before the end of steam with little used 70ft tables which had previously been installed at such unlikely places as Witham and Melton Constable. Kings Cross shed could not turn Pacifics until December 1932 when the turntable seen here was installed, noteworthy at the time as it was worked by vacuum created by the engine's ejector. The A2/3 shows the original type of boiler fitted with a round dome well forward and a return to a flat fronted cab. The Thompson round dome boilers gave trouble with water surging into the steam supply pipe to the engine steam brakes, injectors and ejector, in the latter case with unpleasant results if anyone was standing near the engine as the sooty water was ejected from the chimney. *Photo: R. C. Riley*

A1/1

No.60113 *Great Northern*, after rebuilding by Thompson, at Doncaster depot in April 1958: the solitary example of class A1/1. Although officially a rebuild of the original Gresley Pacific of 1922, No.4470 in 1945, practically nothing from the earlier engine was used, except the tender, some wheel centres and part of the cab. The locomotive was built in the New Erecting Shop at Doncaster whilst the other No.4470 was stripped at the other end of the works, the parts going into the pool to repair other Pacifics. Although much has been made of the selection of *Great Northern* for rebuilding it was intended to renew all the remaining 180 lbs/inch engines, now class A10 with the A4 boiler rather than the A3. *Great Northern* compared well with the A4 in economy and performance and its mileage per annum averaged 55,000 after rebuilding, which was higher than its life as a Gresley engine, despite requiring more visits to main works for attention to the front end. When first rebuilt no smoke deflectors were fitted and the chimney was rimless. The wheelbase and overall length were only exceeded by the Raven Pacifics of the North Eastern Railway when fitted with an eight wheel tender. The weight was the same as the Raven engines at 101tons 10cwts and, oddly, all the Thompson Pacifics except those based on the V2 weighed exactly the same.
Photo: W. Potter

A2

BELOW: No.60532 *Blue Peter* at St Rollox in September 1966, when it was a Dundee engine. The locomotive has been privately preserved and is the only example of the post-war LNER Pacifics to have survived. Although personally I do not like the white or aluminium paint with which this loco is adorned, the electric headlights do show up to advantage.
Photo: W. Potter

LEFT: No.60533 *Happy Knight* ex works at Doncaster shed in May 1956. Both this and *Blue Peter* are fitted with MLS multiple valve regulators inside the smokebox. Five of the A2 class were so fitted in 1949 and at the same time received Kylchap double blastpipes. The fitting of the MLS regulators was experimental at the request of the BRB, to gain experience with this type prior to fitting it to the Britannia Pacifics. The dome now housed a tangential steam drier, a fitting tried earlier by Gresley which had provoked the comment from Bulleid that he could find no way of measuring whether it was of benefit or not!

Happy Knight was the only member of the class to spend its working life allocated to the southern part of the Eastern Region. Originally only one was allocated to Scotland but eventually most of the class were transferred to the Scottish Region in exchange for the disliked A2/2s and for a number of years many worked over the Edinburgh to Aberdeen line for which their high tractive effort was ideal.
Photo: T. B. Owen/Colour-Rail

A2s in service

RIGHT: Peppercorn class A2 No.60534 *Irish Elegance* leaving the Mound Tunnel, Edinburgh, on an Aberdeen express. The 15 A2s were originally ordered by Thompson and would have been class A2/3 but the order was changed to the more compact front end arrangement as soon as the Chief Mechanical Engineer had retired. The divided drive was retained and accommodated by pushing the inside cylinder well forward, increasing the front overhang and using a very short inside connecting rod the same length as in the Thompson Pacifics. Whereas in the Thompson arrangement all the connecting rods were of the same length, in the A2s the outside rods were made longer by almost 3 feet. The 'banjo' steam collector dome reappeared due to the troubles experienced with water surging into the steam supplies on the A2/3 and a partly wedge shaped cab front was used. The latter put the safety valves outside the cab which was a better arrangement, retaining the advantage of the sloping cab windows to avoid reflections. The wedge shaped cab front had been a feature of all the Pacifics and V2s since the A4 until the A2/3 and A1/1. The change back to a single chimney, however, marred the performance of these otherwise very capable locomotives. Many of the Scottish area A2s averaged over 60,000 miles per annum.
Photo: P. M. Alexander, Millbrook House Collection

ABOVE: Peppercorn A1 class No.60139 *Sea Eagle* attaching the Hull portion to a Leeds to Kings Cross express at Doncaster in May 1963. It was a time consuming process for the train engine to haul the three coaches out onto the running line and back onto the rest of the train in the adjoining platform, a task once performed with a shunting engine at the rear.
Photo: Hughes Junction

LEFT: No.60121 *Silurian* ex works on Doncaster shed in May 1963. Note the Smith-Stone speedometer fitted to the trailing coupled wheels, a feature added from 1960. Although the A4s had Flaman speed recorders fitted before the war and while some of the A1 class were also fitted when built in 1948-1949, the Pacifics were generally not fitted with any form of speedometer until 1959 when this type was adopted by British Railways for all express passenger engines.

The A1 class was the final design of the LNER Pacifics and 49 were built just after nationalisation in 1948-1949. Before the war it was thought unlikely that any more of the A4s would be constructed as it was Gresley's view that future locomotives would be required to pull heavier loads at higher speeds and when No.10000 had been rebuilt as a conventional engine a 50 sq ft grate had been used, as adopted in the P2. An outline drawing of a Pacific with this feature and also much larger locomotives with eight coupled wheels had been prepared. During the war and initially afterwards, with heavy loads and generally poorer quality coal, the larger grate was desirable and was therefore used in the new Pacifics built by Thompson and Peppercorn, including the A1 class. In the 1950s the weight of trains was reduced and the emphasis was on accelerated timings but not just for a few selected trains. The A1s spent most of their lives hauling trains well within their designed capacity. At a time when some of the older Pacifics could not be relied upon, the A1 class as a whole performed consistently well, day in day out, running higher mileages than their predecessors and with the lowest maintenance costs by far of any of the class 8 express passenger engines on BR.
Photo: Hughes Junction

ABOVE: No.60131 *Osprey* already without its nameplates heading a Newcastle express in August 1965 out of Leeds, two months before withdrawal. The A1 class were remarkably free steaming engines and it was not usually necessary to emit black smoke on this scale. The A1 and A2 classes were tested in 1949 with the dynamometer car producing excellent results. The average coal consumption in lbs/dhp hour was only slightly in excess of the A4 on its home ground and with the smaller grate, but on one of the test runs the A1 hauling a 490 ton train from Leeds to Kings Cross did so with a coal consumption of 33.86 lbs/ml or 2.694 lbs/dhp hour which was a very good result, and underlined how far Doncaster had progressed over the years in improving the efficiency of the Pacific locomotive.
Photo: J. Richardson

LEFT: A1 class No.60140 *Balmoral* inside one of the roundhouses of York depot on 30th August 1964, a few months before being withdrawn. By 1966 all the A1s had gone after an average life of only 15 years, the last from York depot. The building now forms part of the National Railway Museum.
Photo: Gavin Morrison

BELOW: An unkempt A1, No.60134 *Foxhunter*, is deputising for a failed diesel on the 17.18 Leeds to Newcastle parcels train in August 1965. Many of the A1s still in service were not kept very clean.
Photo: J. Richardson

Last days of the A1s

A close-up of No.60157 *Great Eastern* at Holbeck depot on 17th October 1964. It was withdrawn the following January. The A1 class as a whole were not named when built and *Great Eastern* was not fitted with nameplates until November 1951, the crest being handpainted. The position of the inside cylinder can be seen by the row of bolts on the frames. The bogies on all the Thompson and Peppercorn Pacifics had the weight taken on side bearers, unlike the A4s where the weight was on the centre. The riding of the A1 was not as consistently good as the A4 and the former was more sensitive to track conditions generally. One Kings Cross driver, Arthur Davis, had No.60149 *Amadis* at one period as his regular engine: he said it could pull anything, including the station as well if you wanted to hang it on, but when was I going to stop his engine riding across the fields!

Great Eastern was also a Kings Cross engine at one time and oscillated from side to side at speeds over 60 mph. After examination in works and adjustment to the weight on the bogie side control springs it came back to Kings Cross riding normally. It was one of five engines fitted with roller bearings and went on to run well over 190,000 miles before having to go into Doncaster works for a general overhaul because of broken boiler stays. All the axles were fitted with roller bearings which had been tried on some of the A4 tenders and these were very reliable, giving no trouble whatsoever. All the class were fitted with electric lighting as seen on this engine but many sets were removed over the years. The steam driven turbo-generator was situated behind the smoke deflector on the other side.
Photo: Gavin Morrison

Last glimpse

A1 class No.60148 *Aboyeur* working an up Pullman train on Gamston bank in June 1959. It is an A1 in excellent condition, running well with an absence of smoke and blows. *Photo: Hughes Junction*

ALSO AVAILABLE

The Colour of Steam Vol.5 - London Midland in the Fells
The Colour of Steam Vol.6 - The LMS Pacifics
Other titles in preparation

OUR NEW MAGAZINE

In 1986 Atlantic published the first issue of BACKTRACK, a high quality quarterly devoted entirely to British railway history and incorporating a number of unique features. Each issue includes: 12 large pages of *full colour* historical photographs; an article on *each* of the 'Big Four' railway companies (or respective BR region); a branch line article; plus a wealth of other well-researched material on British railway practice over 150 years up to the mid-1970s. BACKTRACK is on sale in major newsagents and selected specialist railway and model retailers. For a sample copy send £2.25 to the address at the front of this book.